Next Generation ENERGY

LEAVING OUR MARK

Reducing Our Carbon Footprint

Nancy Dickmann

CRABTREE
Publishing Company
www.crabtreebooks.com

Crabtree Publishing Company

www.crabtreebooks.com

Author: Nancy Dickmann

Editors: Sarah Eason and Jennifer Sanderson and Petrice Custance

Proofreader: Katie Dicker

Editorial director: Kathy Middleton

Design: Paul Myerscough and Jessica Moon

Cover design: Paul Myerscough

Photo research: Sarah Eason and Jennifer Sanderson

Prepress technician: Tammy McGarr

Print coordinator: Margaret Amy Salter

Consultant: Richard Spilsbury, degree in Zoology, author and editor of educational science books for 30 years

Production coordinated by Calcium Creative

Library and Archives Canada Cataloguing in Publication

Dickmann, Nancy, author
    Leaving our mark : reducing our carbon footprint / Nancy Dickmann.

(Next generation energy)
Includes index.
Issued in print and electronic formats.
ISBN 978-0-7787-2381-3 (bound).--
ISBN 978-0-7787-2385-1 (paperback).--
ISBN 978-1-4271-1758-8 (html)

    1. Environmental responsibility--Juvenile literature. 2. Sustainable living--Juvenile literature. 3. Energy conservation--Juvenile literature. 4. Greenhouse gas mitigation--Juvenile literature. 5. Environmental protection--Juvenile literature. I. Title.

GE195.7.D53 2016   j363.7   C2015-907827-X
                                      C2015-907828-8

Library of Congress Cataloging-in-Publication Data

Names: Dickmann, Nancy, author.
Title: Leaving our mark : reducing our carbon footprint / Nancy Dickmann.
Description: Crabtree Publishing Company, [2016] | Series: Next generation energy | Includes index. | Description based on print version record and CIP data provided by publisher; resource not viewed.
Identifiers: LCCN 2015045108 (print) | LCCN 2015044046 (ebook) | ISBN 9781427117588 (electronic HTML) | ISBN 9780778723813 (reinforced library binding : alk. paper) | ISBN 9780778723851 (pbk. : alk. paper)
Subjects: LCSH: Environmental responsibility--Juvenile literature. | Sustainable living--Juvenile literature. | Energy conservation--Juvenile literature. | Greenhouse gas mitigation--Juvenile literature. | Environmental protection--Juvenile literature.
Classification: LCC GE195.7 (print) | LCC GE195.7 .D53 2016 (ebook) | DDC 363.7--dc23
LC record available at http://lccn.loc.gov/2015045108

Crabtree Publishing Company

www.crabtreebooks.com   1-800-387-7650

Printed in Canada/012016/BF20151123

Published in Canada
Crabtree Publishing
616 Welland Ave.
St. Catharines, Ontario
L2M 5V6

Published in the United States
Crabtree Publishing
PMB 59051
350 Fifth Avenue, 59th Floor
New York, New York 10118

Published in the United Kingdom
Crabtree Publishing
Maritime House
Basin Road North, Hove
BN41 1WR

Published in Australia
Crabtree Publishing
3 Charles Street
Coburg North
VIC, 3058

Contents

Greenhouse Earth

A layer of gases, called the atmosphere, surrounds our planet. These gases protect Earth by burning up space rocks before they hit the planet, and filtering out harmful radiation. They also keep Earth's temperature warm and constant. Without the atmosphere, it would be too cold for life to exist on Earth.

Earth's atmosphere is made up of about 78 percent nitrogen and 21 percent oxygen. The oxygen in the atmosphere is what allows us to breathe. The remaining one percent is made up of the gases argon, **carbon dioxide**, and water vapor, as well as tiny amounts of other gases.

Although carbon dioxide (CO_2) makes up only about 0.03 percent of the atmosphere, it plays an important role. Plants need carbon dioxide in order to make their food. Carbon dioxide, as well as other gases such as **methane**, also trap the Sun's heat inside Earth's atmosphere. When radiation from the Sun reaches Earth's surface, some of it bounces back. Some radiation will pass harmlessly through the atmosphere. However, if radiation hits **molecules** of CO_2, the molecules will absorb the heat **energy** and trap it in the atmosphere.

Violent storms, such as Hurricane Sandy, could become more frequent as a result of rising temperatures. In other areas, **droughts** will become more common.

Too Hot

Too much CO_2 in the atmosphere traps more heat and causes Earth's average temperature to rise. This is called the **greenhouse effect**. Records show that Earth's temperature has risen slowly but steadily over the last century, and even more quickly in recent years. Even small temperature rises can have a large effect. They can create droughts. They can also bring heavy storms and disrupt ocean currents, which affects **climate**. Warmer temperatures also cause the polar ice caps to melt, which raises sea levels. The rising sea levels could cause coastal cities to flood. All of these changes to the usual pattern of weather are known collectively as global **climate change**.

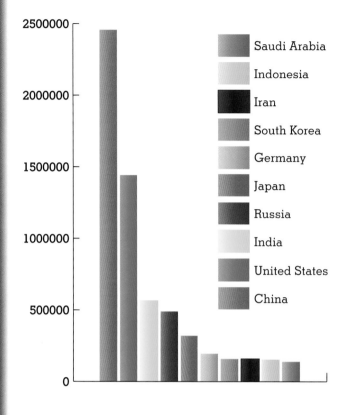

Top 10 Carbon-producing Countries 2011

- Saudi Arabia
- Indonesia
- Iran
- South Korea
- Germany
- Japan
- Russia
- India
- United States
- China

Many of the biggest carbon-producing countries have huge populations. This graph shows how many metric tons of carbon each country produces.

FAST FORWARD

Rising sea levels could be a real problem for many low-lying nations. Scientists estimate that if climate change continues at the same pace, land on which 100 million people currently live will be underwater within a century. Do you think that people would take more decisive action against climate change if their own homes were at risk? Give reasons for your answer.

What Is a Carbon Footprint?

You may have heard carbon footprints mentioned in the media. What exactly does this term mean? A carbon footprint is a measurement of the amount of **greenhouse gases** put into the atmosphere by the activities of a person or group of people. Greenhouse gases contribute to the greenhouse effect and the warming of Earth. To calculate your own carbon footprint, you add up the **emissions** of all the lifestyle choices you make.

Carbon dioxide is the main greenhouse gas, but others, such as methane and nitrous oxide, are also included in carbon footprints. A carbon footprint is often expressed in kilograms or metric tons with the unit **CO_2e**, which is short for carbon dioxide equivalent. It is a measure of the amount of CO_2 that would have the equivalent global warming impact.

Take something as simple as buying a book. The factory that printed the book will have emitted greenhouse gases while making it. More gases were emitted by the truck that carried the book to the store where you bought it. Did you go by car to the bookstore or did a delivery van bring the book to your house? Both trips create more emissions.

Even an activity as simple as sending a text message contributes to your carbon footprint. Electricity is used to send the message.

What about the author, who used electricity to power the computer as he or she wrote the book? A fraction of those emissions can be assigned to every copy that is sold.

Inexact Science

As you can see from this example, calculating an exact carbon footprint is difficult. You can find many carbon calculators online that ask questions about things like energy use in your home and your travel habits. They can give you an approximate idea of what your carbon footprint is, but it will just be an estimate. The more detail taken into account, the more accurate an estimate is likely to be.

Every product you use had to be made. Manufacturing products always causes some CO_2 emissions.

REWIND

Today, the world's CO_2 emissions are 150 times higher than they were in 1850. This is partly because the world's population is so much larger. However, it is also due to **industrialization**. Factories pump CO_2 into the air when producing consumer goods. Our lifestyles have also changed, and we take for granted things such as car and air travel. The world's population will only continue to increase. What sort of lifestyle changes do you think are needed to stop climate change? Explain your answers.

Where Gases Come From

Methane is emitted in smaller quantities than CO_2, but it has a greater warming effect. Over 100 years, one ton of methane causes the same warming effect as 25 tons of CO_2. Nitrous oxide, which can be emitted by using fertilizer, has 300 times the warming effect.

The majority of CO_2 emissions come from burning **fossil fuels** such as oil, coal, and natural gas. We burn fossil fuels in vehicles, as well as in factories and power stations. Carbon dioxide from fossil fuel use makes up about 57 percent of all greenhouse gas emissions.

Another significant source of greenhouse gases is **deforestation**. When land is cleared for agriculture or **industry**, a lot of the plants are burned. This releases carbon dioxide. Even natural events such as forest fires and the decay of plant matter are significant sources of CO_2. There is another downside to losing forests. Trees actually absorb CO_2. Not only does the destruction of trees release CO_2 into the atmosphere, it also takes away a natural means of removing CO_2 from the air.

Oil is used to make products such as gasoline that release CO_2 when burned. Significant amounts of other greenhouse gases are also released during the process of drilling for oil.

Emissions by Sector

You can also study greenhouse gases by the activities that lead to their production. The production of electricity and heat for use in homes and businesses accounts for 26 percent of greenhouse gas emissions. Burning fossil fuels in power stations creates most of these emissions. Industry is next, accounting for 19 percent. This includes fuels burned on site at factories and other industrial locations, such as mines and refineries. Agriculture makes up 14 percent, which includes methane released by livestock. Transportation is responsible for 13 percent. Other sources of greenhouse gases include the treatment of waste and wastewater, which also releases methane and other gases.

Cows may look harmless, but they are a big contributor to the greenhouse effect. An average cow releases 26 to 53 gallons (98.4 to 200.63 liters) of methane each day as a result of belching and flatulence.

REWIND

Fossil fuels such as oil, natural gas, and coal were formed millions of years ago from the remains of living things that were buried. These organisms contained carbon, so the fossil fuels they turned into still contain that carbon. The carbon is released when they are burned. There are ways to generate electricity that do not release carbon, such as by wind, solar, and **hydroelectric power**. Do you think alternative energy sources will become more important in the future? Why do you think they may or may not?

Getting the Full Picture

Looking at your own carbon footprint is a good way to visualize the effect your lifestyle has on the planet. However, it is incredibly difficult to calculate the exact carbon footprint of any one person, product, or activity. Greenhouse gases can be released at any stage during the manufacturing, shipping, or use of a product.

Think about driving to the grocery store. This is something that your family probably does at least once a week. It is fairly easy to calculate the amount of gas the car burns during the trip. This falls into the category of "direct emissions." However, there are a lot of "indirect emissions," too. Greenhouse gases were created when the car was built in the factory, and a tiny slice of these can be assigned to each journey the car makes over its lifetime. In addition, the extraction, refining, and transportation of the gasoline the car uses all create emissions, too.

Buying second-hand goods helps you save money and reduces carbon emissions produced by waste. When you do not want things any more, sell or donate them instead of throwing them away.

Everything Has a Footprint

Think about a gadget such as a cell phone. Greenhouse gases were released when it was manufactured and shipped. What about the company that made it? Its designers, engineers, and sales team used energy when they worked on it in a well-lit, heated office. All of this CO_2 affects the planet, regardless of where it came from in the production process.

Nearly everything, however small or insignificant, has a carbon footprint. If you want to help fight climate change, you need to think about the carbon impact on the planet whenever you make a decision about what to buy or do.

Recycling produces less carbon than making new items from scratch. For example, companies can reuse the plastic in a bottle, instead of manufacturing new plastic.

The Energy Future: You Choose

One scientist estimates that the emissions involved in producing a pair of jeans and transporting them to a store is about 13 pounds (6 kg) CO_2e. That is roughly equivalent to an 8-mile (12.87 km) drive in an average car. It may not sound like a lot, but how many pairs of jeans do you have in your closet? Following fashion often means buying new clothes before your old ones wear out. Is that more important than reducing your carbon footprint? Give reasons for your answer.

Around the World

Around the world, people's lifestyles are very different. So are their carbon footprints. In some countries, the carbon emissions per person are much lower than in other countries. Economics and lifestyle choices play a big role in this.

The five countries with the highest overall levels of carbon emissions are China, the United States, India, Russia, and Japan. China and the United States have much larger footprints, but this could be due to their higher populations. When you divide a country's emissions by the number of people living there, the figures look very different. For example, India's emissions per person are just 1.7 metric tons, which is fairly low. China's are 6.7 metric tons per person. Some developed countries are significantly higher. Russia's emissions are 12.6 metric tons per person, while Canada (14.1) and the United States (17.0) are even higher.

On this map, the shapes and sizes of the countries have been distorted so the ones with the highest carbon emissions look bigger than they really are.

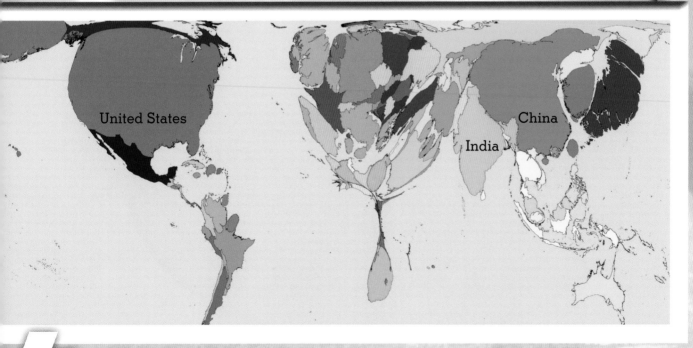

United States

India

China

Why So Different?

In richer, more developed nations, carbon emissions tend to be higher. In these countries, many people can afford larger homes with electricity, heating, and sometimes air conditioning. A large percentage of households have at least one car, and people are used to being able to buy consumer goods.

In less developed countries, this is often not the case. The economies of many poorer nations are improving due to their increased production of goods and services, which in turn helps to increase their citizens' standards of living. As their standards of living increase, their carbon footprints also get bigger. People in both developed and less developed nations need to cut their carbon footprints dramatically.

In China, many families can now afford a car for the first time. Although there are many cars on the road in China, the United States still has higher vehicle ownership per citizen.

The Energy Future: You Choose

Most carbon statistics look at how much carbon is actually emitted in a particular country from manufacturing, travel, electricity, or other sources. However, some scientists think we should also consider the carbon impact of things we **import**, or buy in, from other countries. For example, many products are manufactured in China and shipped around the world. China's emissions are very high, but they would be lower if they were not manufacturing goods for the rest of the world. What do you think is the best way to add up carbon emissions? Explain your answer.

Carbon Offsets

Carbon offsetting is a method of canceling out some of the carbon emissions we create by paying a fee. This money is used to help reduce emissions in other areas. Carbon offsets can be purchased to offset something as small as a train or airplane journey, or to offset much larger things, such as the activities of entire businesses.

The idea behind a carbon offset is to cancel out the effect of a product or activity by reducing emissions somewhere else. These reductions can take many different forms. They might involve companies giving out low-energy light bulbs, planting trees, or **investing** in research into **renewable** energy, such as wind power.

For example, if you are going on a long plane trip, you can cancel out the journey's carbon footprint. First you must choose an offsetting company. Then you use its online calculator to find out what your personal emissions will be for the flight. This is translated into a fee for you to pay. The offsetting company will use your fee to reduce carbon emissions in some way.

Trees have to be planted in the right areas to have a positive effect on climate change. It is just as important to keep the forests we already have.

Who Offsets?

Anyone can choose to offset their emissions, but currently companies and governments do most of the carbon offsetting. They often have to follow strict limits on carbon emissions. For example, some countries have signed an international agreement called the **Kyoto Protocol**, which gives them emission targets that they must stay below. If a country looks like it is going to emit more carbon in a year than it is allowed, it can buy credits from a country that will emit below its limit. One country is buying the right to emit more, and the other country is paid for emitting less. This way the global carbon balance is maintained.

Sometimes, money from carbon offsetting is used to help build wind or solar energy farms.

FAST FORWARD

In the early days of carbon offsetting, a lot of money went into planting trees. An average mature tree can absorb about 50 pounds (22.68 kg) of CO_2 per year. That is roughly equivalent to the amount of CO_2 emitted during a 10-mile (16.09 km) drive in heavy traffic. There is simply not enough space to plant the amount of forests needed to absorb all of the carbon we emit. How do you think the money from carbon offsets could be better spent?

How Low Can We Go?

In the United States, the yearly **per capita** carbon emissions are about 17 metric tons CO_2e. This is higher than many other countries. For example, in the European Union, the figure is just 6.8 metric tons CO_2e. Although smaller, this amount is still too high. Many scientists believe we must get emissions down to at least 2 metric tons CO_2e per capita to stop climate change.

The Kyoto Protocol is an international agreement that was reached in 1997. Countries that signed up to the protocol agreed to work to cut their carbon emissions. Many promised they would cut their emissions in the period from 2008 to 2012 by an average of 5 percent compared to their emissions in 1990. Additionally, they promised to cut their emissions in the period from 2013 to 2020 by 18 percent compared to their 1990 levels.

However, not all countries have signed the Kyoto Protocol. For example, the United States and China have not signed. Canada signed at first, but after a change in government, it became the first country to withdraw from the agreement in 2011. Some countries are not hitting their targets but are trading energy credits with other countries to make up for it. In the first period, the 37 countries with targets cut their overall combined emissions. However, emissions in other countries increased.

When sea temperatures rise, coral reefs are bleached, or turned white. This makes the coral far more vulnerable to disease.

How Will We Do It?

Countries can achieve lower emissions by passing laws that require businesses to be more carbon efficient. They can invest in cleaner energy to reduce the use of fossil fuels. They can also plan new communities in more **energy-efficient** ways using new building techniques and organizing towns so that people do not have to drive as much to get goods and services.

Many people around the world think that governments are not doing enough to reduce greenhouse gas emissions.

FAST FORWARD

Do you think you could cut your personal carbon emissions in half within five years? Think about the changes you would have to make. Turning off lights or switching to energy-saving light bulbs will make a small difference, but you will need to think big. Do you go by plane when you go on vacation? Do you regularly upgrade your cell phone or computer? How often do your parents drive you places? How much are you willing to cut to reduce your footprint? Give reasons for your answers.

Green Transportation

If you want to reduce your carbon footprint, there is a range of different changes you can make. One of the biggest contributors to an individual's footprint is transportation. You may not yet drive, but you still have a lot of options for reducing your emissions.

For short journeys, walking or cycling are the most carbon-efficient ways to travel. You will save money and get valuable exercise. Experts say that biking for half an hour a day can increase your life expectancy by about four years. If you attach a basket or other carrier to your bicycle, you will be able to use it for shopping or carrying your books to school.

If you live in a large town or city, public transportation such as buses, subways, or trains may be an option. On average, a bus or train releases more carbon than a car. However, these emissions are split between all the passengers, so the emissions are lower per person.

In the past, buses were a significant source of greenhouse gases. Now, newer designs mean that they are much cleaner, though many older buses are still on the roads.

Driving

There are some trips where driving is necessary, so talk to your parents about car usage. You may be able to drive less by carpooling with friends or combining errands to save trips. There are also ways of driving that use less fuel, such as accelerating, or increasing speed, gently. This will save money as well as lower your family's emissions. When it is time to replace your family's car, look for one that is fuel efficient, such as a hybrid gas-electric model. You could even think about using a car-sharing program instead of owning a car.

Many cities, such as Boston, have introduced bicycle-sharing programs. Users pay a fee to pick up a bike, ride to their destination, and drop it off.

The Energy Future: You Choose

Traveling by airplane can hugely increase your carbon footprint. A flight lasting 5 hours can add as much as 1 metric ton CO_2e to your footprint. That is a huge percentage of the recommended target of 2 to 5 metric tons per year. For some journeys, you could take a train instead. If you do not want to give up flying, keep it to a minimum. How could you change your vacations to make them more carbon-efficient? Give examples to support your answers.

A Low-Carbon Home

Our homes are another big source of carbon emissions. We use huge amounts of energy to keep our homes warm in the winter and cool in the summer. Even more energy is used to keep homes well-lit and comfortable. However, some fairly small changes can have a big impact on your home's carbon footprint.

You probably do not have much control over the thermostat in your house, but it is worth having a family discussion about ways to reduce the bills. Installing better **insulation** can help keep your home's temperature comfortable all year round. In the winter, simple things like hanging thick curtains and closing them at night can cut heat loss through windows.

A lot of our electricity is produced by burning fossil fuels, so using less electricity is important. Switching to energy-efficient light bulbs is a good start. Turn off lights when you are not using them and use natural light where possible. You should also turn off appliances when you are not using them. Many types, including televisions, have a "standby" mode that uses electricity even when the device is off. Unplugging these devices will stop the energy flow. Newer models of electronic devices waste less energy than older models, but it is still worth turning them off when you can.

In many places, old-fashioned incandescent bulbs are being phased out. They waste a lot of energy. Newer light bulbs are often more expensive, but they last longer and use less energy.

Hot Water

Purifying and heating up tap water both leave carbon footprints. That means saving water also reduces carbon emissions. Take short showers instead of baths, and turn the faucet off while you brush your teeth. Use the dishwasher or washing machine only when you have a full load to cut down on the number of times you run them. You may also be able to use a cooler temperature setting on these machines.

Wearing an extra layer of clothes and using blankets can mean that the thermostat does not need to be turned up higher.

The Energy Future: You Choose

Not all appliances are created equally. Some have a much bigger carbon footprint than others. When it is time to replace your family's television, refrigerator, washing machine, or other appliance, help do the research to find the most energy-efficient models. They may cost a little more but could save your family money in the long run. What do you think should be the most important factor when choosing an appliance? Explain your answer.

Shopping

The products we buy, and where they come from, have a big impact on our carbon footprint. In the clothing industry, for example, greenhouse gases are emitted throughout the design, manufacturing, and shipping processes. The stores that sell consumer goods also create emissions by lighting and heating the stores, and by their employees who must travel to work.

One of the simplest ways to reduce your carbon footprint is to buy less. Do your research and look for well-made products that will last, instead of needing to be replaced quickly. Buy second-hand or vintage, or even swap with your friends when you want something new. This advice could apply to clothes, books, gadgets, and much more.

So much of what we buy is wrapped in paper or plastic packaging. Greenhouse gases are emitted when the packaging is manufactured, and we often throw it away as soon as the item is unwrapped. Some packaging can be **recycled**, which reduces emissions. Say no to plastic bags and carry a reusable one instead. If you think a product has too much packaging, write to the store or the manufacturer and ask them to use less.

New clothes have a big carbon footprint, so think about shopping at a second-hand store instead. You might find something unique.

Is Online Better?

These days, we can buy anything online, including food, clothes, and books, and have them delivered directly to our homes. Is buying online more energy-efficient than shopping in person? Delivery trucks and vans burn a lot of fuel, but they deliver to multiple homes on each trip. Studies have shown that unless the store is fairly close to your house and you get there by foot or public transportation, it is greener to shop online.

Worldwide, we use an average of 150 disposable plastic bags per person per year. Many stores encourage shoppers to bring their own bags by charging them for plastic bags.

The Energy Future: You Choose

Many people use shopping as a leisure activity, but buying a lot of new things adds to your carbon footprint. There are many other activities with less impact. Go for a bicycle ride with your friends or play soccer in the park. Work on art or craft projects and use recycled materials! Can you think of any other ways to have fun with a low carbon impact?

Communication

It is natural to want to stay in touch with one another, and modern technology makes it easier than ever before. From text messages to video calls, there are a huge number of ways to keep up with friends and family. Communication is not something you can touch or feel, so it is easy to forget that all these activities come with their own carbon footprint.

When you use your cell phone to send a text message, you use up part of your phone's electric charge. Your friend does the same when he or she reads it and responds. In addition, the cell phone network uses electricity to send the signal. However, it all adds up to a pretty small amount. Using the phone to talk creates much higher emissions. Calls from a landline and text messages are definitely the lowest-carbon options.

It costs less than a penny to charge your phone, but transmitting calls across the network uses a lot more energy. Talking for an hour a day on can add up to more than 1 metric ton CO_2e in a year.

Computers

Sending an email is also fairly low-carbon, as long as it is a simple message with no large attachments. Sending an old-fashioned paper letter has a much bigger footprint because there are emissions involved in the manufacturing of the paper as well as the cost of delivering it.

A lot of communication takes place through computers. Both manufacturing the computer and powering it contribute to its carbon footprint. However, the websites that we use depend on huge data centers. This is where all the digital information you find on websites, including videos and music, is stored. The servers in these data centers use a lot of electricity. They also produce a lot of heat, so even more electricity is used to keep them cool.

Every time you use the Internet to shop, research, watch videos, or play games, you are creating emissions at a data center.

The Energy Future: You Choose

It is good to want to talk to your friends, but we sometimes rely on technology instead of face-to-face contact. The emissions caused by sending photos, videos, or music, or by video chatting can really add up. It is so easy to hit "forward" or "share" when we see something we like, but think before you click. Is there a lower-carbon way of getting your message across?

Maximum Impact

Reducing greenhouse gas emissions is a challenge that the whole world needs to tackle. It is such a big problem that many people wonder if their own efforts can possibly make enough of a difference. With new coal-fired power stations still being built and pumping out greenhouse gases, many people wonder if something as small as switching off the lights really matters.

There are more than 7 billion people in the world. Each of us makes choices about what to buy and what to do. If enough people change their habits, even by a small amount, it can still add up and make a big difference. For example, the average person could cut his or her carbon emissions by about half a metric ton per year just by reducing packaging waste by 10 percent. Imagine the effect if millions of people did that.

If enough people worldwide make small changes in their daily lives, the effects will add up.

Think Big

Even though small changes can add up, you still need to focus on the activities where you can make the biggest impact. You may wonder if it is better to use paper towels or an electric dryer to dry your hands in a public bathroom. The carbon difference between the various options is pretty small, but you should still choose the greenest one (a high-powered, non-heated electric dryer) if you can. However, you cannot congratulate yourself on doing your part to fight climate change if you still upgrade your cell phone each year, eat meat every day, or fly more than once a year. These activities have a much bigger effect on your overall carbon footprint.

Being a regular flier can cancel out many low-carbon lifestyle changes that a person may make.

FAST FORWARD

Ten or twenty years from now, living a low-carbon lifestyle may be second nature. New homes could be built from recycled or natural materials, with plenty of insulation. Their roofs could be covered with plants to absorb carbon dioxide, or solar panels to provide electricity. Smart technology and more energy-efficient appliances could keep electricity from being wasted. However, even the greenest house cannot control the decisions of the people living in it. The choice is yours: what changes will you make to reduce your carbon footprint?

Power Up!

Cutting your carbon emissions may seem like extra work but it has definite benefits. By using and wasting less, your family can save money. Some lifestyle changes, such as riding a bike instead of taking the car, can improve your health. By knowing that you are doing something to help the world, you will feel better, too.

What Can You Do?

There are countless groups working to fight climate change. Why not get involved? You do not have to be an adult to make a difference. Anyone can write to politicians and business leaders, asking what they are doing to lower emissions. You could also petition your local government, encouraging them to think about environmental issues when they decide how to use land or what to build. Get your whole family involved in lowering your household's emissions. You can use an online calculator to estimate your current carbon footprints, then work together to make a plan for lowering them. Keep track of your progress and see how low you can go!

Talk to your parents about spending decisions and help them make choices that will save your family money as well as reduce your carbon footprint.

Activity:

Before you can make plans to cut your carbon footprint, you need to find out how big it is. By identifying the areas of your life where the biggest emissions are, you can find ways to make a real difference.

You Will Need:

- Computer with Internet access
- Pen
- Paper

Instructions

1. Find an online carbon footprint calculator. There is a link to a good one on page 31.
2. Fill in the information to figure out your carbon footprint. You can do this for just yourself or for your whole family.
3. Identify the areas where you or your family has the biggest footprint. For example, it may be heating and cooling, electricity, transportation, or food and cooking.
4. Research ways to cut your carbon footprint in each of these areas.
5. Talk to your family and suggest changes you could make. Set targets for the next month and agree on a reward for hitting the targets.
6. Keep track of your results.

What Happened?

Were you able to hit your targets? How easy was it? You may be able to go even lower in the next month. Or, you could choose a different area to focus on. Talk to your friends about what you have been doing and see if you can persuade any of them to try the challenge in their own homes.

My Carbon Footprint Reduction Goals

	Week 1 Reduction	Week 2 Reduction	Week 3 Reduction	Week 4 Reduction
Heating				
Electricity				
Transportation				
Food				

Glossary

Please note: Some bold-faced words are defined where they appear in the text

atmosphere The layer of gases that surround Earth

carbon dioxide A gas molecule made of a carbon atom joined with two oxygen atoms

climate The normal weather conditions that an area has over a long period of time

climate change Changes to the usual weather patterns in an area or the entire Earth

CO_2e Short for "carbon dioxide equivalent." A unit of measure that translates greenhouse gas emissions into the equivalent amount of carbon dioxide.

deforestation Cutting down or burning all the trees in an area

droughts Long periods of time with lower than average rainfall

economics The process or system by which goods and services are produced, sold, and bought

emissions Things released or given out. For example, greenhouse gases are emitted when fossil fuels are burned.

energy The ability to do work. Energy can take many different forms

energy-efficient Operating or working in a way that gets results with little wasted energy

fossil fuels Energy sources made from the remains of plants and animals that died millions of years ago and were buried

greenhouse effect When atmospheric gases allow the Sun's energy to reach the surface, but prevent energy reflected off the surface from going back into space

greenhouse gases Gases, such as carbon dioxide and methane, that contribute to the greenhouse effect

hydroelectric power Electricity generated from the energy of moving water

import To buy in

industrialization The increased use of machines to do work

industry The making or producing of goods or services

insulation Materials used to stop heat, cold, or electricity from escaping

investing Giving money to help develop a product or idea, in the hope that it will eventually earn enough to pay back the money

Kyoto Protocol A document signed by state parties that commits them to reduce greenhouse gas emissions

manufacturing Making something on a large scale using machinery

meteorites The remains of rocks or metals that fly through space to reach Earth's surface

methane A hydrocarbon molecule made up of one carbon atom and four hydrogen atoms. It is a greenhouse gas.

molecules The smallest units of a substance that have all the properties of that substance. A molecule can be made up of atoms of a single element, or atoms of two or more different elements

offsetting The process of canceling out carbon emissions by paying for reductions in emissions elsewhere

per capita Per person

radiation Waves of energy sent out by sources of heat or light, such as the Sun or by radioactive substances

recycled Something used again, either for the same purpose or by turning it into a new product

renewable Something that renews itself once it is used

Learning More

Find out more about carbon footprints and how to make yours lower.

Books

Dutton, Michael. *Amazing Carbon Footprint Facts*. Dover Publications, 2010.

Green, Dan. *Climate Change* (Basher Science). Kingfisher Books, 2015.

Hunter, Nick. *How Carbon Footprints Work* (Ecoworks). Gareth Stevens, 2013.

Sneideman, Joshua and Erin Twamley. *Climate Change: Discover How it Impacts Spaceship Earth* (Build it Yourself). Nomad Press, 2015.

Websites

This calculator helps you see how much carbon you could save by making simple changes in your daily life. You can use it for the activity on page 29:
www3.epa.gov/climatechange/kids/calc/index.html#calc=instructions

NASA's climate site has some useful tips for reducing your carbon footprint at:
http://climatekids.nasa.gov/review/how-to-help

If you are interested in a career in environmental science, this website has a lot of useful information:
www.bls.gov/ooh/life-physical-and-social-science/environmental-scientists-and-specialists.htm

Index